Withdrawn

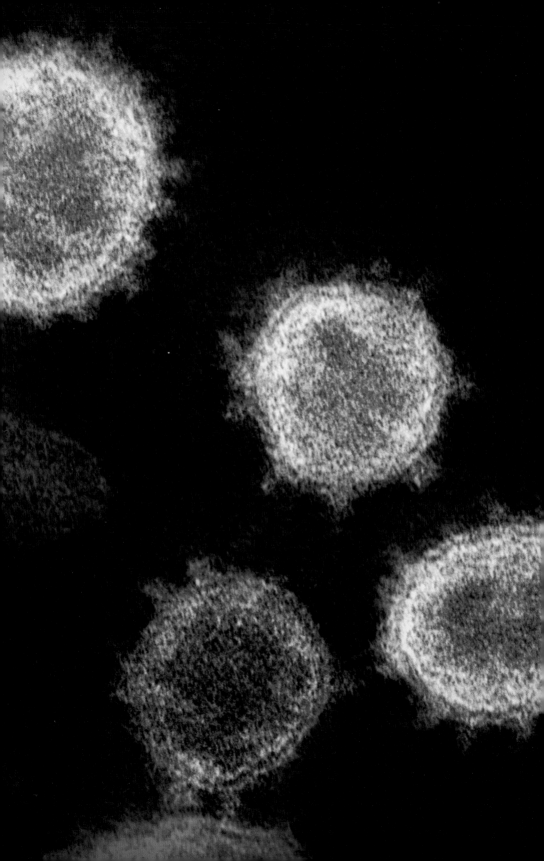

THE COVID PANDEMIC

ODYSSEYS

RACHAEL HANEL

CREATIVE EDUCATION · CREATIVE PAPERBACKS

Published by Creative Education and Creative Paperbacks
P.O. Box 227, Mankato, Minnesota 56002
Creative Education and Creative Paperbacks are imprints of
The Creative Company
www.thecreativecompany.us

Design and production by Blue Design (www.bluedes.com)
Art direction by Rita Marshall

Photographs by Getty (Yuichiro Chino, South China Morning Post, Spencer
Platt), iStock (alvarez, chriss_ns, FreeTransform, gerenme, littleny, Derek Yung),
Pexels (Fatih Turan), USHHS (Chandler West), USAFRICOM (Staff Sgt. Devin
Nothstine), U.S. Department of Defense (Bill Evans, Petty Officer 3rd Class
John Hig), Unsplash (Yoav Aziz, Clay Banks, Brittani Burns, Comparefibre, Joel
Muniz, Brett Wharton), Wikimedia Commons (Gustavo Basso, Hamilton Henry
Dobbin, NIAID-RML, Mike Pence, Tim Reckmann, St. Louis Post Dispatch, U.S.
Center for Disease Control)

Library of Congress Cataloging-in-Publication Data
Names: Hanel, Rachael, author.
Title: The COVID pandemic / by Rachael Hanel.
Description: Mankato, Minnesota : Creative Education/Creative Paperbacks,
   [2023] | Series: Odysseys in recent events | Includes bibliographical
   references and index. | Audience: Ages 12-15 | Audience: Grades 7-9 |
   Summary: "Teens explore the history of the COVID-19 pandemic from a
   journalistic viewpoint to understand how the virus spread and its effect
   on the world"-- Provided by publisher.
Identifiers: LCCN 2022015476 (print) | LCCN 2022015477 (ebook) | ISBN
   9781640267152 (library binding) | ISBN 9781682772713 (paperback) | ISBN
   9781640008564 (ebook)
Subjects: LCSH: COVID-19 Pandemic, 2020---Juvenile literature. | COVID-19
   (Disease)--Social aspects--United States--Juvenile literature.
Classification: LCC RA644.C67 H36 2023 (print) | LCC RA644.C67 (ebook) |
   DDC 614.5/92414--dc23/eng/20220506
LC record available at https://lccn.loc.gov/2022015476
LC ebook record available at https://lccn.loc.gov/2022015477

CONTENTS

Introduction

In December 2019, it was business as usual at the Huanan Seafood Wholesale Market in Wuhan, China. The noisy market was bustling with people who picked through a dazzling array of fruits and vegetables in every color. Shoppers could also buy fresh fish and meat. In some cases, chickens were butchered on the spot.

OPPOSITE: Live animal markets in China sell a variety of animals for food or as pets, from chickens to hedgehogs, bamboo rats to snakes.

What people didn't know as they went about their shopping: a virus was lurking among them, ready to unleash unimaginable devastation. No country would be left untouched by the virus's effects.

ealth experts believe that the virus responsible for COVID-19 is connected to the food market in Wuhan. Caged wild animals in the market likely carried the disease and transmitted it to people. What is known: From Wuhan, the virus spread rapidly around the world. In just over two years, six million people died. The pandemic changed the way society lived and had a lasting impact on the world.

COVID-19 testing sites used nasal swabs and saliva collection to check people for the virus.

A Mounting Fear

Human beings have always lived with pandemics, sometimes known as plagues. "What happened in 2020 was not new to our species. It was just new to us," said medical expert Nicholas Christakis. Viruses surround us every day. Many are carried by birds or wild animals. But sometimes they escape their animal hosts and infect a human, who in turn spreads it to other people. One of the deadliest pandemics in history was the bubonic plague.

OPPOSITE: The Great Plague of Marseilles, France, in 1720, was the port city's deadliest, killing about 45,000 people (about half the city) over a two-year period.

A medical team attends to influenza victims in 1918.

Versions of this plague appeared in the years 541, 1665, and 1743. However, the version that reached Europe in 1347 was especially deadly. It is known as the "black death," and it killed an estimated one-third of the European population.

In the modern era, the influenza (flu) pandemic that began in 1918 killed an estimated 50 million people around the world over the course of two years. Many of those who died were young adults in their twenties and thirties. Influenza continued to infect large numbers of people in 1957, 1968, 1976, and 2009, but not as many as the 1918 pandemic or the recent COVID-19 pandemic.

Health experts have always worried about the next pandemic. In 2003, people in Asia started to get very ill, and many died. Doctors diagnosed the illness as severe acute respiratory syndrome (SARS), a type of coronavirus. However, SARS ended shortly after it began. Another coronavirus called Middle Eastern Respiratory Syndrome (MERS) appeared in 2012. It infected many people, mainly in the Middle East. This illness was very deadly.

Government officials in the United States believed it was only a matter of time before a pandemic would invade the world again. In 2005, President George W. Bush read a book about the 1918 influenza outbreak and worried about another pandemic affecting the country. He assembled a team of eight medical experts to prepare a pandemic plan. The plan had three parts:

C., July 29.—The
leave Washington
ugust 15, owing to
t. He will confer
aniels probably to-
easibility of hav-
eet await his ar-
ng San Francisco

CHICAGO
RAILWAY
S STRIKE

evated Systems
ity Tied Up
alk-out

IGHER WAGES

ents and Eight
Demand 85,
Boost

29.—Fifteen thou-
employes went on
wages at 4 o'clock
letely tying up the
ed systems of the
y made no attempt
kers had to depend
ways, automobiles
o reach their pla-

the heads of the
cials of the street
reached an agree-
ges of the men at
cents an hour and
y with time and a
. It was thought
ert a walkout, but
shortly before mid-
ed to strike at 4
mployes demanded
an increase of 77
sent wages, an 8-
e and a half for

ARD TO
NEWEST
SCHEME

oses Effort to

mission will enter a
ehalf of North Da-
conference to be
tomorrow against

SWAT THE FLU IS SLOGAN FOR
1919 CAMPAIGN AGAINST DREAD
DESTROYER THAT AGAIN LOOMS

Measure Introduced in Both Houses of Congress Would Appro-
priate $5,000,000 for Investigation of Epidemic Which Swept
Over America in 1918, Costing Thousands of Lives.

HELP FIGHT THE FLU
By asking the congressman
from your district, and the sen-
ators from this state, to work
for and vote for the anti-flu bill
introduced in congress by Senator Harding and Congressman
Fess.
THERE IS URGENT NEED
FOR HASTE.
A recurring flu epidemic is
feared this autumn and winter.
It may be more serious than the
one of 1918.
Fighting the flu NOW may head
off the epidemic. It will save
lives.
WRITE TO WASHINGTON
THIS EVENING.

N. E. A. Washington Bureau.
Washington, D. C.—Congress is being told plainly, clearly, and straight-
from home, that the people want their
government to get busy immediately
in a nation-wide campaign to head off
a recurrence of the dread influenza
epidemic.
Letters and telegrams by the thousands are coming to members of both
houses urging them to work for and
vote for the Harding-Fess bill which
appropriates $5,000,000 for influenza
investigation.
This measure is the first step in a
comprehensive and effective fight on
the flu. It proposes to do what can-
not be done otherwise, for it places
the United States government in
command and back of the anti-flu
fight. And it proposes to keep the
government there until after the flu
germ has been tracked to its lair, and
its ravages upon human life is an-
cient history.

**UNDER DIRECTION OF
U. S. HEALTH SERVICE.**
The Harding-Fess bill, if it be-
comes a law, would place the United
States Public Health Service in direct
charge of the anti-flu fight. This service would cooperate with the medical
departments of the navy and army,
and with other public and private research laboratories that have facili-
ties for assisting in the work.
Senator Warren G. Harding and
Congressman Simeon D. Fees, both of
Ohio, introduced the bill, but the
"father" of the measure is the American Medical association, which at its
annual convention, urged the neces-
sity of a governmental appropriation
and investigation of influenza in this
country. The medical association's
anti-flu stand has been warmly sup-

SEN WARREN G. HARDING

THE FLU BILL.
A measure introduced in both
houses of congress to set aside
$5,000,000 for investigation of
the influenza epidemic, its cause,
methods of prevention, and the
cure.
The bill was introduced in the
Senate by Senator Warren G.
Harding, and in the house of rep-
resentatives by Congressman Simeon D. Fess, both of Ohio.
The money appropriated is to
be spent under the direction of
the United States Public Health
Service.
The measure is endorsed by the
American Medical association.

ND. FESS

EATH TOLL.
lled in the United
States in the last four months of
1918—470,000 human beings.
Influenza killed in the United
States during the recurring epidemic of this spring—50,000 hu-

come to individual members of congress urging the passage of the anti-
flu bill.
OTHER LEGISLATION

Twenty-four Killed and Man
Raged Since Sunday Ev
Angry Mobs—Tro

Chicago, July 29.—Four
stood ready today to quell ra
during two nights of terror
of at least 22 men, including
dreds of others, many serio
the injured are soldiers. T
to make a complete statem
20 were killed last night.
A hundred thousand neg
in the streets, or alleys, or
Mounted police galloped alon
the streets with prisoners an
men fought with cudgels, kr

STOCKYARDS ARE
PACKERS LEVER
UPON LIVESTOCK

Manipulation of Markets on
Part of Big Five Charged
by Commission

Washington, D. C., July 29.—Manip-
ulation of livestock markets by control of yards and practical monopoly
in the buying of livestock was charg-
ed against the "Big Five" packers in
the third section of the federal trade
commission's report on the packing
industry, just made public.
The report cited data obtained in
the investigation to show that the
"Big Five" held a majority of voting
stock in 22 of the principal stockyards
of the country and interest in the re-
maining 28.
"Of the meat trade in the hands of
interstate slaughterers in the U. S."
said the report, "the five packing
companies have more than 73 per cent
of the total. They have the prices of
dressed meat and packing house products so well in hand that within certain limits meat prices are made to
respond to their wishes."

LAWYERS' TAGS COME
HIGH COMPARED WITH
LADY PUPS AND JACKS

"It seems to me when we consider
the license fee on female dogs and

drow
of th
night
The g
Burli
Dicks
fall t
the ci
night
the lo

hund
rapid
forme
Prope
of th
14 w

Ther
foren
order
14 wl

possi
in So
were

11 o
were

AN

The Young and the Sick

Typically, influenza affects the elderly and very young children more seriously. The 1918 pandemic behaved differently: It affected young adults, ages 20 to 40, including many young men who were fighting in World War I (1914–1918). Medical experts are still not sure why this was the case. One theory is that their strong immune systems set off an over-reaction to the infection. This over-reaction resulted in a build-up of fluid in the lungs that often leads to deadly pneumonia.

1) detect outbreaks overseas and keep them contained; 2) develop and obtain plenty of vaccines and medicines to fight viruses; and 3) develop a plan of action at local, state, and federal levels. Bush got the ball rolling for pandemic planning. But when he left office in early 2009, the presidents after him focused on more pressing issues, such as the economy, health care, and foreign wars. Pandemic planning took a back seat.

That pandemic team and other health experts were watching China closely in December 2019 and January 2020. The first COVID-19 patient was diagnosed in Wuhan on December 1, 2019. That person did not have any connection with the Huanan Seafood Wholesale Market, but two-thirds of the first 41 COVID-19 patients did. The market shut down on January 1, 2020. Due to the Chinese government's tight control of negative information, the world did not know at first how serious the virus was. As the number of cases grew, Chinese officials started to release information. The entire country shut down on January 25 to try to control the outbreak, but it was too late. Infected people had already traveled outside of China. The virus was now spreading around the world at a frightening rate.

Usually, the deadlier the disease, the slower the transmission. A severe disease is usually detected early. People are isolated quickly to be treated, or they die quickly before the virus has a chance to spread. On the

COVID-19 is 10 times deadlier than seasonal influenza.

other hand, viruses that are not as deadly affect a higher percentage of the population. People walk around with mild symptoms and spread the virus to others. Think of the common cold. It spreads easily and rapidly, but generally people do not get seriously ill or die.

COVID-19 was different. The illness caused by this new virus usually starts off mild, but it can turn deadly quickly. It causes severe respiratory illness and is a coronavirus related to SARS and MERS. COVID-19 is 10 times deadlier than seasonal influenza. Common symptoms of COVID-19 are a headache, congestion, dry cough, and loss of taste or smell. In severe cases, COVID-19 causes chest pain

In March 2020, then-vice president Mike Pence addressed emergency teams in Washington, one of the states hardest hit by COVID-19.

and difficulty breathing. It is tough to diagnose and treat because half of those who are infected show no symptoms. These asymptomatic people have the virus but may not realize it, so they may unknowingly spread the virus to others.

The first case of COVID-19 in the U.S. was reported to the Centers for Disease Control on January 21, 2020. The infected man was from Snohomish, Washington, and had traveled back home on January 15 after visiting Wuhan. He had not been at the Huanan market, and he had not come into contact with anyone displaying symptoms. He likely received the virus from an asymptomatic person. Health officials started to screen passengers coming into the United States from Wuhan, but only at the largest airports such as New York, Los Angeles, and San Francisco.

In February and March of 2020, many people were becoming infected on cruise ships. On board, people from around the globe lived in close quarters, making it easier for the virus to spread. The *Grand Princess* ship left San Francisco on February 11. By March 11, the virus had been detected in 78 people—some were passengers, while others were people who had contact with infected passengers once the ship docked. Another cruise ship, the *Diamond Princess,* was forced to dock in Yokohama, Japan, in early February. All 3,711 people aboard were quarantined and not allowed to disembark. At least 712 people aboard contracted the virus, and 12 of them died.

On March 11, 2020, the World Health Organization (WHO) declared COVID-19 a global pandemic because of how fast the disease was spreading. The world was about to go into lockdown.

Six Feet Apart

The early days of the pandemic introduced the concepts of physical and **social distancing**. People were told to stay at least six feet (1.8 m) away from each other in public places such as grocery stores. At that distance, larger droplets expelled from the mouth or nose tended to fall to the ground, according to scientific studies. Social distancing meant that people were to stay at home as much as possible and refrain from getting together with people outside of their households.

The World Reacts

Soon after WHO declared the pandemic, countries around the world had to decide how to keep the virus from spreading. Most countries ordered lockdowns and cancelled large events such as conventions. By mid-March, many states in the U.S. and provinces in Canada went on lockdown. Business offices closed, and people worked from home.

OPPOSITE: As the pandemic spread around the world, maps that indicated hot spots (places where the numbers of COVID-19 cases were highest) were a common sight.

Bars and restaurants closed. Visitors were not allowed into nursing homes, deeply affecting family relationships. And in one of the more controversial decisions, schools closed. Teachers delivered lessons through videos to students at home. People everywhere got used to logging onto a video platform called Zoom for school, work, family visits, and worship.

The message was clear: "We need to be very serious ... for a while, life is not going to be the way it used to be in the United States," said Dr. Anthony Fauci, a member of

President Donald Trump's virus task force and a leading infectious disease expert. "We have to just accept that if we want to do what's best for the American public."

These dramatic restrictions were put into place in an attempt to "flatten the curve." If a large number of people got sick at the same time, health care systems would be overwhelmed. Hospitals would run out of space. Doctors, nurses, and other medical staff would be so busy treating COVID-19 patients that they might not be able to focus on other patients. But if virus transmission could be slowed, health care systems would be better equipped to treat the sick. Studies showed that lockdowns saved lives.

In some places, the shutdowns came too late. Italy was the first country to suffer enormous loss. In the early days of the pandemic, Italian officials underestimated

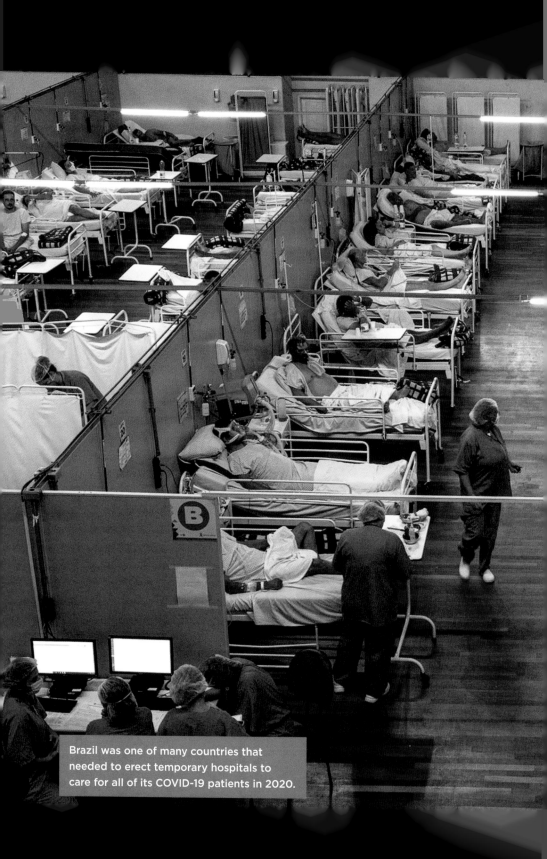

Brazil was one of many countries that needed to erect temporary hospitals to care for all of its COVID-19 patients in 2020.

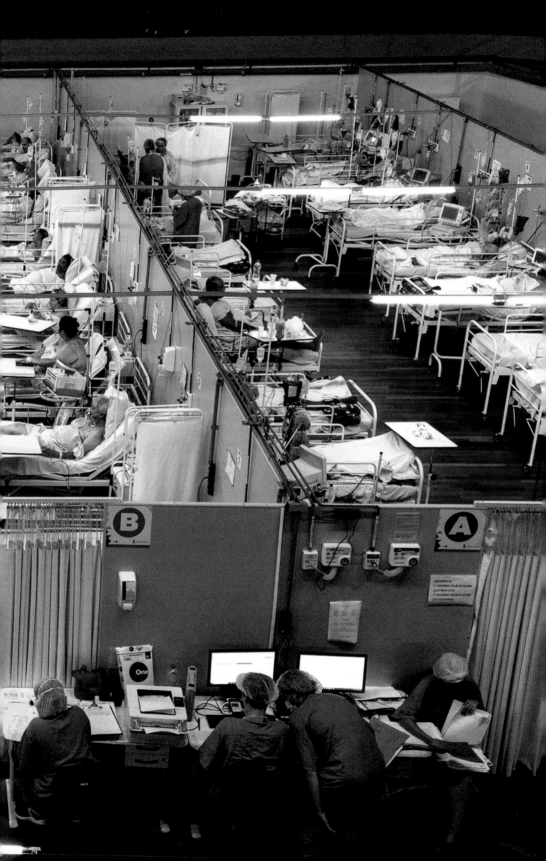

the severity of the virus. By the time lockdowns were ordered, the virus was raging throughout the country. In New York City, health care workers ran out of personal protective equipment such as masks and gowns in April 2020. Intensive-care units (ICUs) filled up quickly with people who had severe symptoms. It became hard to find room for patients who were suffering from non-COVID-19 emergencies.

Health care workers were among the essential workers who could not work from home. Gas stations, grocery stores, hospitals, and clinics stayed open. Fire and police services were still needed. Garbage still had to be picked up. Goods still had to be packaged, shipped, and delivered. Construction projects continued. These workers put their own health at risk so others could be safe, warm, and fed. One worker at a grocery store in Queens, New

York, said, "My job was to make sure other families can eat." It was estimated that 30 million people worked in essential jobs in 2020, according to the Center for Economic Policy and Research.

Countries, states, and cities could institute lockdowns, but people also took individual responsibility to slow the spread of the virus. These efforts are known as non-pharmaceutical interventions (NPI). These included washing hands, social distancing, and wearing masks. Masks help stop the spread of disease. When people talk, cough, sneeze, or sing, tiny droplets and particles are expelled from the mouth and nose. These particles might carry the virus in asymptomatic people. A mask barrier reduces the number of particles that reach other people. This is why doctors and nurses wear masks in operating rooms. Masks also keep people from touching their faces, which is another way the virus spreads. "Even if masks reduced the transmission rate of the virus by only 10 percent, our models indicate that hundreds of thousands of deaths would be prevented around the world. . . ." Christakis said.

Despite the lockdowns and NPI, the virus gained a worrisome foothold in the United States. In just over three months, the country had two million cases. In a little over six months, there were nearly 6.7 million cases. It became impossible to test everyone with symptoms

Who Is Dr. Anthony Fauci?

Dr. Anthony Fauci has been a leading researcher on diseases for more than 50 years, but COVID-19 has made him a household name. He retired from government in December 2022. Over the span of his career, he served as Chief Medical Advisor for seven U.S. presidents. In early 2020, President Donald Trump chose Dr. Fauci to serve on his coronavirus task force. Dr. Fauci told the American people, in simple terms, how the virus worked and what we could do to protect ourselves and others. Dr. Fauci was the director of the National Institute of Allergy and Infectious Diseases from 1984 to 2022. He was one of the leading researchers in the 1980s on the virus HIV, which causes the disease AIDS. He helped develop medicines that allowed some people with HIV to live long and productive lives.

or to do contact tracing to find people with whom an infected person had contact while contagious. Contact tracing requires a lot of time to track everyone's movements. Testing can identify those who have the virus, but widespread testing was not available in the early days of the pandemic.

The decisions regarding who got tests and whether to require masks were left to state and local governments. This resulted in a patchwork of different rules across the United States. Immediate mandates went into effect in many cities and states in efforts to flatten the curve. The mandates required restaurants and bars to close their indoor dining, banned large gatherings, and required people to wear masks while in public. Some people did not agree with these mandates. Across the country, groups protested in their state capitols. At one

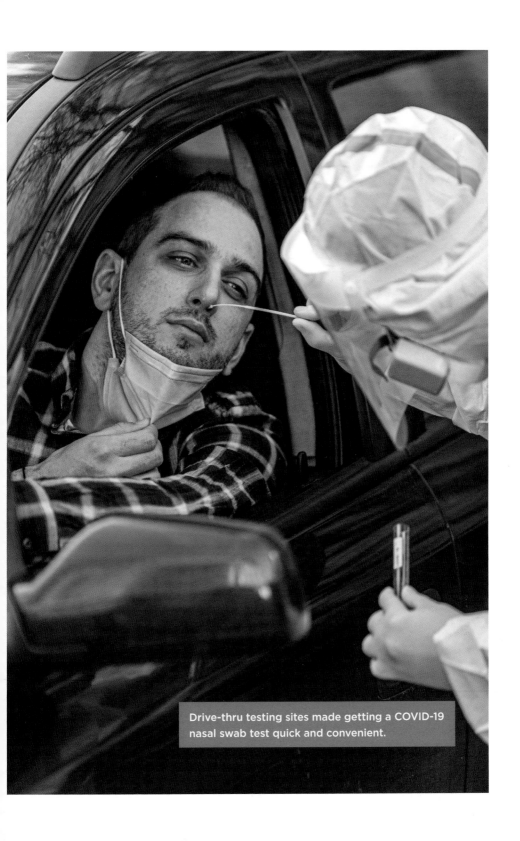

Drive-thru testing sites made getting a COVID-19 nasal swab test quick and convenient.

COVID-19 affected people of all ages and ethnicities. But it more seriously affected the elderly and people of color.

event in Michigan, armed protestors entered the state capitol building. At an event in Minnesota, state troopers stood guard between those for and against mandates. Some governors did not create any statewide mandates. In those states, cities and counties had to make their own decisions on what businesses to shut down or create their own masking policies.

COVID-19 affected people of all ages and all ethnicities. But it more seriously affected the elderly and people of color. In the U.S., those over the age of 65 accounted for about 75 percent of all deaths. Studies showed that

Black, Hispanic, and American Indian/Alaska Native populations were twice as likely to die from COVID-19 than white people.

A s the pandemic continued, people were worried and anxious about how their cities and states were handling the outbreak. They turned to the media to stay informed about hot spots and the latest guidelines. During lockdowns, a television, newspaper, or online news site became one of people's only sources of information about the outside world. Public health

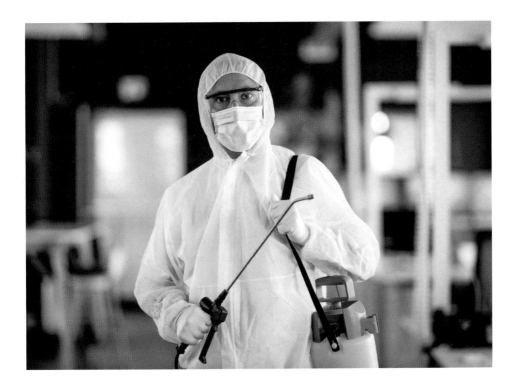

officials used the media to communicate important information, such as how COVID-19 spreads and what people can do to stay safe. However, it became difficult to find accurate information, especially on social media. During lockdown, social media use increased 87 percent. It was easy for rumors and unscientific information to spread and hard to find reliable information, which

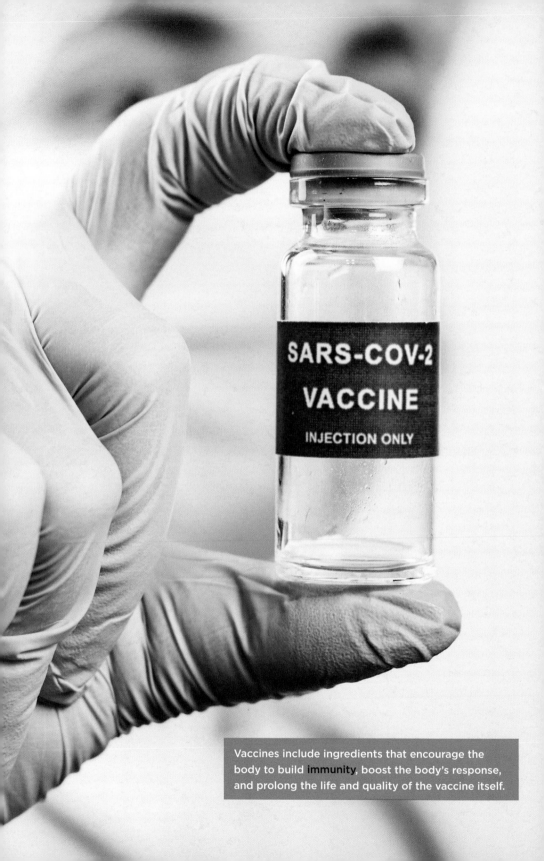

Vaccines include ingredients that encourage the body to build **immunity**, boost the body's response, and prolong the life and quality of the vaccine itself.

contributed to uncertainty. Rumors started to spread about "miracle" treatments for COVID-19.

At the same time, scientists and researchers were working to develop a vaccine against COVID-19. More than 100 trials were underway by May 2020. A headline in *The New York Times* on May 20, 2020, read "A New Entry in the Race for a Coronavirus Vaccine: Hope." What many people didn't know was that scientists and researchers had been working on a coronavirus vaccine for many years. The threat of SARS in 2003 and MERS in 2012 had prompted the medical community to begin vaccine research years ago. The Trump administration made the development of a vaccine in 2020 a priority. Operation Warp Speed, with billions of dollars in funding for vaccine research, was underway. There indeed was hope on the horizon.

Triumphs and Setbacks

Of the more than 100 vaccines being researched, only a few made it to the important clinical trial phase. In this phase, tens of thousands of people volunteered to receive vaccines so scientists could understand how they worked in the body. The trials were conducted through the summer and fall of 2020, and the highly successful results were even better than scientists had hoped for.

The company Moderna enrolled 30,000 people in its clinical trial. The company found that two doses of the vaccine resulted in an efficacy rate of 94.1 percent. That meant that 94.1 percent of people in the trials didn't contract the virus when they were exposed to it. The people who did get sick had only mild symptoms. The vaccine had helped their bodies make antibodies to fight against it. The Pfizer vaccine trials showed similar results. About 95 percent of the people who had received the two vaccine doses did not contract the virus. Johnson & Johnson created a one-dose vaccine. Their trials showed an 85 percent efficacy rate.

Usually, vaccines take years to create. Thanks to the prior research done by scientists on previous coronaviruses, the COVID-19 vaccines were rolled out in months. On December 8, 2020, the first vaccine was given to a grandmother in the United Kingdom. Margaret Keenan's birthday was the next week, and she called it the "best early birthday present." In the United States, nurse Sandra Lindsay received the first vaccine dose on December 14, 2020. The first groups of people to receive vaccines were health care workers, people over age 65, and those with conditions that made them more likely to get seriously ill. By spring 2021, vaccines were authorized to all adults 18 and older. Pfizer expanded its vaccine to include those ages 16 and 17.

Though many people celebrated the rollout of the vaccines, not everyone wanted a shot. Concerns over the safety of vaccines have existed for years. Some parents choose to not vaccinate their children for measles or mumps. For the COVID-19 vaccine, the rapid development concerned some people. They weren't sure it was

Herd Immunity

When people get sick or are vaccinated against a disease, they build up an immunity against the virus. When the majority of a population has immunity, the virus no longer easily spreads. This is known as herd immunity, which is often expressed as a percentage. For COVID-19, estimates vary on when a community will achieve herd immunity—the number of people who have either been infected and recovered, as well as those vaccinated. Some scientists think it is 70 percent, some think it is higher. Because COVID-19 is so new, it is not certain if we will ever reach herd immunity.

safe to take. Others didn't want the shot because they already had contracted COVID-19 and thought that natural immunity would protect them. Some worried about the ingredients in the vaccines. Many women were concerned that they would experience problems getting pregnant. Health officials said that data from the vaccine trials, in which tens of thousands of people received the shots, showed the vaccines were safe.

Once vaccines were widely available, places such as universities, large businesses, nursing homes, hospitals, and major sports venues required people to get vaccinated.

Controversy erupted over these requirements. Some people could not get the COVID-19 vaccine due to medical reasons or chose not to for religious purposes.

As vaccines started to roll out in early 2021, COVID-19 still posed many difficult challenges. The disease affected everyone in some way, and the emotional toll was heavy. Health care workers witnessed heartbreaking scenes day after day. Visitors were still banned from hospitals and nursing homes. Seriously ill patients, many near death, suffered alone.

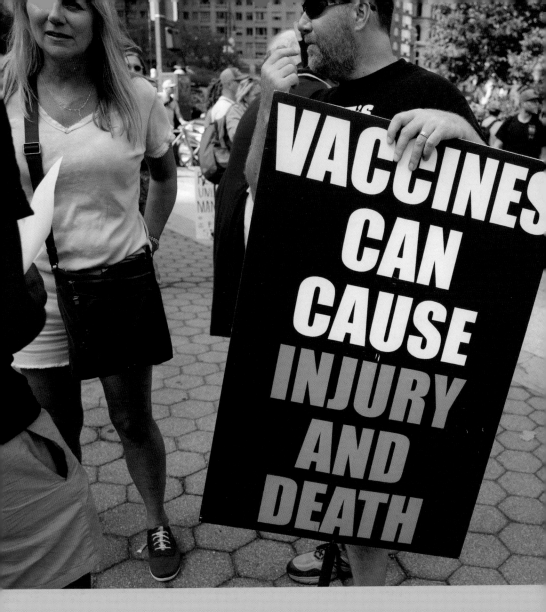

The Spread of Misinformation

When news of the coronavirus first emerged, some people had different ideas of where the virus came from and how it behaved. These ideas were not supported by research or science. This misinformation spread quickly through the internet and social media. One rumor said the COVID-19 vaccine had a microchip inside to track people. Another said the vaccine changed one's DNA. Other people believed the vaccine was responsible for new variants or for causing the large number of deaths. Health experts used scientific evidence to fight these false claims.

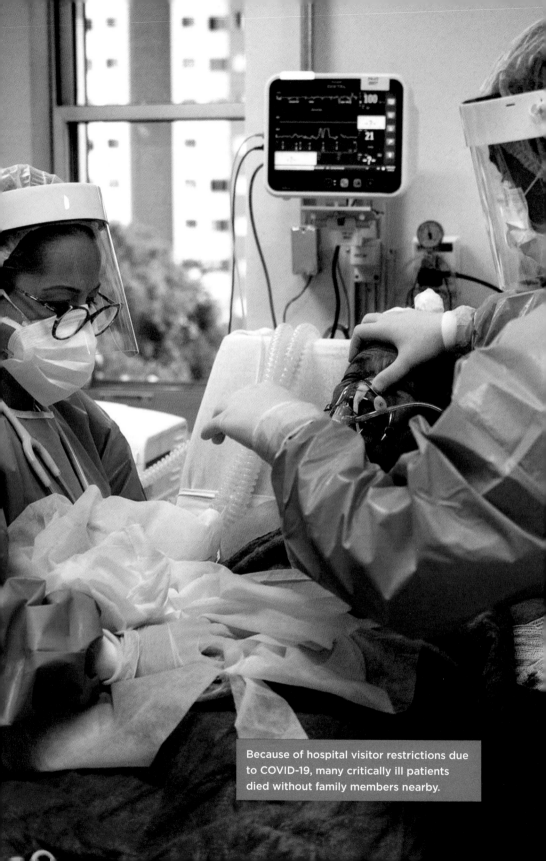

Because of hospital visitor restrictions due to COVID-19, many critically ill patients died without family members nearby.

Often, the only person who could be in a room with a dying patient was a nurse, doctor, or aide. Jennifer Kay Jensen of Delray Beach, Florida, could not be with her husband as he was dying of COVID-19. "The guilt, it eats me up every day," she said. "I think it could have made a difference, if I was there seeing him, to soothe him or scratch his arm or kiss his head."

any funerals were delayed until it was safer to gather. Families who chose to have funerals for their loved ones had to limit attendance, and people had

"It's terrible seeing families sitting six feet apart, not able to reach out to each other."

to practice social distancing. No one could hug or offer other physical support of sympathy. "It's terrible seeing families sitting six feet apart, not able to reach out to each other," said Lianna Champ, a funeral director in the United Kingdom. "And can you imagine how awful it is choosing who attends a funeral?"

Many people lost their jobs. When the world went into lockdown in March 2020, the unemployment rate spiked from 3.5 percent to 14.8 percent, the highest level ever recorded. That meant about one out of every seven people eligible to work did not have a job. People slowly started to return to work, but the unemployment rate was still at 5.4 percent in 2021.

Schoolchildren around the world struggled with remote learning. "Going to school used to excite me but sitting in front of a computer for eight hours a day does not interest me. I wish we could go back, even one day a week. Even one day a month. Even in small groups. I don't really care," said Fiona O'Toole, a ninth grader in Chicago. Schools were also an important way for many children to receive healthy meals. Children could not always get enough to eat at home. In addition, not every home had internet access. Distance learning made it impossible for many children to keep up.

Some people faced physical challenges. Studies suggested that up to 30 percent of people who contracted COVID-19 suffered health effects for months. This is known as "long-haul" COVID-19, or long COVID.

In July 2022, New York City relaxed its mask mandate but still required masks on public transportation and in health care settings.

Those effects can include extreme fatigue, difficulty breathing, headaches, nausea, or the inability to walk. "I used to be a healthy and strong member of the Air Force, and now I struggle to lift anything over five pounds. This has honestly been a very scary journey. I don't want anyone else to experience what I'm going through," said Isaiah Smith of California, who was just 26 years old when he got sick.

As the pandemic continued, the media and politicians received increasing criticism. Some people thought the media was blowing the pandemic out of proportion. Critics lashed out at politicians. Governors who imposed mask mandates were criticized. Governors who did not impose mask mandates also were criticized.

OPPOSITE A COVID-19 spin on the classic tale of Little Red Riding Hood

Public health officials at state and local levels took the most criticism. Often it was these state and local officials who had to decide what protections to put into place. Some officials received harassment through phone, email, and social media. People went to their homes to threaten them.

Dr. Anthony Fauci became the face of health information for the entire country. Some people saw him as a good guy, and some saw him as a bad guy. Frank Bruni of *The New York Times* said, "Fauci isn't perfect. But he has been perfectly sincere, perfectly patient, a professional standing resolutely outside so many of the worst currents of American life. More than that, he has been essential." Kathleen Parker of *The Washington Post* disagreed. She wrote, "[Fauci] has ceased to be as

„Grandmother, why do you have no mask on?"

effective as we need him to be in the information battle against COVID-19."

As the world battled the virus, it was becoming more and more apparent: The virus would change the world and how we live forever.

A Changed World

There's no doubt that the COVID-19 pandemic has changed the way people live. While some changes were temporary, other changes became permanent. For example, there are more remote working options. Many businesses realized that employees were just as productive working from home, and businesses saved money by not renting office spaces.

OPPOSITE: Many post-COVID-19 pandemic workplaces shrank, going from multi-floor office buildings to individual computer screens, with employees working and conducting meetings online.

Many workplaces now offer flexible work schedules, which let workers decide what days and hours they work. All of this flexibility is a benefit to workers. They have more freedom to move closer to family or find a better place to live.

While many mask mandates were lifted once COVID-19 infection rates fell, some people have made masking part of their everyday lives. Mask-wearing has been common in parts of Asia ever since the SARS outbreak of 2003. Whenever there is a surge of illnesses, or they feel sick, a person

Farm to Table Troubles

The disrupted **supply chain** resulted in a ton of food waste. While demand for food at grocery stores and food banks rose, the food service industry took a dive as schools, hotels, and restaurants shut down. Meat processing plants were hit particularly hard. Workers suffered high rates of illness. Nearly 90 percent of the U.S. meat-processing plants had COVID-19 outbreaks in 2020 and early 2021. The short-staffed plants couldn't keep up with production, and farmers had to **euthanize** livestock due to overcrowded farms. The dairy and egg industries also declined. Farmers ended up dumping millions of eggs and gallons of milk that otherwise would have been consumed by diners and schoolchildren. Fresh produce was left to rot in the fields because there were no buyers. Some products were able to be diverted to local food banks or used in community-supported agricultural programs that sell local, organic produce straight to consumers.

Countries with the means to do so, such as the United States, came together and delivered medical supplies to countries in need during the COVID-19 pandemic.

might wear a mask to protect others. COVID-19 made it clear how vulnerable some people are to infection, such as the elderly or those who have weak immune systems.

While the virus affected every part of the world, some countries fared better than others. Countries that had strong health care systems and social support systems fared the best. But countries in areas such as Latin America and the Caribbean faced higher COVID-related deaths. Countries that had already experienced pandemics

Travel restrictions helped stop the coronavirus from infecting new places.

such as SARS or MERS understood the importance of testing and isolating ill people early on in the pandemic. Singapore, South Korea, and United Arab Emirates were able to control the virus in the beginning. These are also countries in which citizens tend to trust and obey their government leaders.

Travel restrictions helped stop the coronavirus from infecting new places. Many countries required travelers to quarantine for several days upon arrival, and they had to show a negative test before they could leave quarantine. Some countries also required travelers to show proof of vaccination. Masks were required on public transportation, including trains and airplanes.

The world also experienced problems with the global supply chain due to labor shortages and increased demand.

Empty store shelves were a common sight during the pandemic, especially for essential items such as cleaning supplies, toilet paper, and paper towels.

Factories in Asia and Europe—major manufacturing hubs—were hit hard by the coronavirus. They were shut down for weeks, and when they opened back up, many operated with a shortage of workers due to people getting sick. This caused a ripple effect. They had to catch up on back orders while trying to fulfill new orders. Americans were buying at a record pace to make life at home easier. From new electronics and office furniture to appliances and home improvement supplies, online shopping spiked. Money that used to go toward services was now going toward home entertainment. Spending on hard goods grew by more than 25 percent from January 2019 to August 2021.

Home delivery services became more popular. Early in 2020, food delivery businesses such as GrubHub and DoorDash struggled to find customers. Then the pandemic hit. Online ordering was convenient and allowed people to avoid trips to grocery stores and restaurants. Instacart and DoorDash expanded their delivery services, and Uber shifted focus to its UberEats business. Food delivery was a lifeline for restaurants that were closed to in-person diners. It also become a way of life for many people.

n the summer of 2021, it looked like the pandemic was receding in many countries. Restaurants opened to indoor dining, some concert venues booked shows, and people cautiously gathered with each other

With mandates against indoor dining during the pandemic, many restaurants added patios, tents, and other outdoor seating to stay in business.

again. But by fall, a new form of COVID-19 started affecting people. This form was more contagious, and it spread quickly around the globe. Case numbers and deaths started to increase. This new form of COVID-19 was a variant called delta.

It is not uncommon for viruses to change form and create a variant. Viruses need a host to survive. When people get vaccinated or become immune, the virus may change to stay alive. Around November 2021, another, even more contagious variant emerged: omicron. This variant spread like wildfire. However, it caused milder symptoms than previous variants and resulted in fewer hospitalizations and deaths.

The variants showed that the effectiveness of the original vaccines was wearing off. Breakthrough cases of variants were affecting even vaccinated people, though their symptoms were generally milder than those of the unvaccinated. Doctors authorized booster shots. In November 2021, children in the United States ages 5 to 11 were approved to receive the COVID-19 vaccine. The first updated booster for adults was rolled out in September 2022. It was meant to target COVID-19 variants.

Experts think COVID-19 will always be with us. Just as the 1918 influenza pandemic left us with strains of flu that we battle every year, the COVID-19 pandemic may leave us with continuous strains of COVID-19. Annual booster shots may become the norm. "Nevertheless, each successive wave—barring serious and unexpected mutations in the virus—will, if history is a guide, be smaller and smaller. The COVID-19 pandemic will eventually end," Christakis wrote. After a pandemic comes the endemic phase, when the virus infects people at a static rate. In this phase, there usually aren't surges or out-of-control transmission rates. The immediate danger recedes, but those who are likely to become extremely ill still take precautions. Life going forward means living with this virus and its variants.

There is no question that COVID-19 turned the world on its head and affected everyone in some way. But we learned a lot about how to protect ourselves during times of illness. We can be grateful for the scientists and researchers who developed vaccines that keep us safe. COVID-19 leaves us with many lessons that can help us weather future pandemic storms.

Going Greek

Variants of COVID-19 that cause a high risk of infection are given different names to help track them. They are named after letters of the Greek alphabet, such as delta and omicron. This naming system allows the public to easily say and remember the different variants. The World Health Organization came up with the naming system as an alternative to naming each variant after the place it was first detected. Officials used to be afraid to report variants because they didn't want the variants to be associated with their country.

Selected Bibliography

Burleigh, Nina. *Virus: Vaccinations, the CDC, and the Hijacking of America's Response to the Pandemic.* New York City, N.Y.: Seven Stories Press, 2021.

Center for Systems Science and Engineering at Johns Hopkins University. "COVID-19 Dashboard." https://coronavirus.jhu.edu/map.html.

Centers for Disease Control and Prevention. "COVID-19." https://www.cdc.gov/coronavirus/2019-ncov/index.html.

Christakis, Nicholas. *Apollo's Arrow: The Profound and Enduring Impact of Coronavirus on the Way We Live*. New York City, N.Y.: Little, Brown Spark, 2021.

Lewis, Michael. *The Premonition: A Pandemic Story*. New York City, N.Y.: W. W. Norton & Company, 2021.

Mahmood, Selina. *A Pandemic in Residence: Essays from a Detroit Hospital*. Cleveland, Ohio: Belt Publishing, 2021.

National Institutes of Health. "COVID-19 Research." https://covid19.nih.gov.

World Health Organization. "Coronavirus Disease (COVID-19) Pandemic." https://www.who.int/emergencies/diseases/novel-coronavirus-2019.

Glossary

antibody | a blood protein produced by a person's immune system to fight disease

asymptomatic | displaying no signs of an illness

authorize | to give permission

congestion | stuffiness in the nose, throat, and chest that makes breathing difficult

contact tracing | the process of attempting to identify people who were in contact with someone diagnosed with an infectious disease

controversial | relating to or causing much discussion, disagreement, or argument

efficacy | the power to produce a desired result or effect; effectiveness

endemic | restricted or limited to a certain region

essential worker | a person with a job that provides services and goods that are necessary to people's health and well-being

euthanize | to painlessly put an animal to death

immunity | protection against a particular infection or toxin

infectious | capable of being passed to someone else by germs that enter the body

intensive-care unit | an area in a hospital reserved for seriously ill patients; often abbreviated ICU

mandate	an official order to do something
pandemic	an outbreak of disease that spreads to multiple countries or continents
quarantine	to isolate for a period of time to prevent a disease from spreading to others
remote learning	the education of students who are not physically present at a school; also known as distance learning
respiratory	related to the lungs and the breathing system
social distancing	the physical space maintained between individuals in social contexts
supply chain	the sequence of steps and processes to produce and deliver goods to a consumer
transmission	the act or process by which something is passed from one thing to another
vaccine	a substance injected into a body to protect against a particular disease
variant	a subtype of a microorganism that is genetically distinct from a main strain but not different enough to be a new strain
virus	an extremely small particle that causes a disease and that spreads from one person or animal to another

World Health Organization (WHO)
a division of the United Nations that responds to worldwide health concerns and emergencies

Websites

CDC: Myths and Facts About COVID-19 Vaccines
https://www.cdc.gov/coronavirus/2019-ncov/vaccines/
　　facts.html
Read common myths that people believe about COVID-19
　　vaccines and the facts that debunk them.

**Columbia Public Health: Epidemic, Endemic, Pandemic:
　　What Are the Differences?**
https://www.publichealth.columbia.edu/public-health-now/
　　news/epidemic-endemic-pandemic-what-are-differences
Learn the differences between these three words and what
　　factors lead to a disease outbreak.

**John Hopkins Medicine: Coronavirus at a Glance:
　　Infographic**
https://www.hopkinsmedicine.org/health/conditions-and-
　　diseases/coronavirus/coronavirus-facts-infographic
Find basic information on the virus that causes COVID-19.

WHO Coronavirus (COVID-19) Dashboard
https://covid19.who.int/
View stats on COVID-19 cases by country.

Index